Auth

This book features 100 influential and inspiring quotes by Ralph Waldo Emerson. Undoubtedly, this collection will give you a huge boost of inspiration.

1

"To be yourself in a world that is constantly trying to make you something else is the greatest accomplishment."

2

"For every minute you are angry you lose sixty seconds of happiness."

3

"Finish each day and be done with it. You have done what you could. Some blunders and absurdities no doubt crept in; forget them as soon as you can. Tomorrow is a new day. You shall begin it serenely and with too high a spirit to be encumbered with your old nonsense."

4

"It is one of the blessings of old friends that you can afford to be stupid with them."

5

"What lies behind us and what lies before us are tiny matters compared to what lies within us."

6

"Always do what you are afraid to do."

7

"Do not go where the path may lead, go instead where there is no path and leave a trail."

8

"I cannot remember the books I've read any more than the meals I have eaten; even so, they have made me."

9

"Live in the sunshine, swim the sea, drink the wild air."

10

"The purpose of life is not to be happy. It is to be useful, to be honorable, to be compassionate, to have it make some difference that you have lived and lived well."

11

"What you do speaks so loudly that I cannot hear what you say."

12

"When it is dark enough, you can see the stars."

13

"Is it so bad, then, to be misunderstood? Pythagoras was misunderstood, and Socrates, and Jesus, and Luther, and Copernicus, and Galileo, and Newton, and every pure and wise spirit that ever took flesh. To be great is to be misunderstood."

14

"Make your own Bible. Select and collect all the words and sentences that in all your readings have been to you like the blast of a trumpet."

15

"The glory of friendship is not the outstretched hand, not the kindly smile, nor the joy of companionship; it is the spiritual inspiration that comes to one when you discover that someone else believes in you and is willing to trust you with a friendship."

16

"All I have seen teaches me to trust the Creator for all I have not seen."

17

"The earth laughs in flowers."

18

"It is easy in the world to live after the world's opinion; it is easy in solitude to live after our own; but the great man is he who in the midst of the crowd keeps with perfect sweetness the independence of solitude."

19

"It is not the length of life, but the depth."

20

"The only person you are destined to become is the person you decide to be."

21

"Whatever you do, you need courage. Whatever course you decide upon, there is always someone to tell you that you are wrong. There are always difficulties arising that tempt you to believe your critics are right. To map out a course of action and follow it to an end requires some of the same courage that a soldier needs. Peace has its victories, but it takes brave men and women to win them."

22

"Dare to live the life you have dreamed for yourself. Go forward and make your dreams come true."

23

"Write it on your heart that every day is the best day in the year."

24

"Once you make a decision, the universe conspires to make it happen."

25

"Adopt the pace of nature: her secret is patience."

26

"Without ambition one starts nothing. Without work one finishes nothing. The prize will not be sent to you. You have to win it."

27

"Cultivate the habit of being grateful for every good thing that comes to you, and to give thanks continuously. And because all things have contributed to your advancement, you should include all things in your gratitude."

28

"Life is a journey, not a destination."

29

"Make the most of yourself... for that is all there is of you."

30

"If we encounter a man of rare intellect, we should ask him what books he reads."

31

"Nothing great was ever achieved without enthusiasm."

32

"A great man is always willing
to be little."

33

"Be silly. Be honest. Be kind."

34

"Be not the slave of your own past - plunge into the sublime seas, dive deep, and swim far, so you shall come back with new self-respect, with new power, and with an advanced experience that shall explain and overlook the old."

35

"Though we travel the world over to find the beautiful, we must carry it with us, or we find it not."

36

"Don't be too timid and squeamish about your actions. All life is an experiment. The more experiments you make the better."

37

"You cannot do a kindness too soon, for you never know how soon it will be too late."

38

"The only way to have a friend
is to be one."

39

"Shallow men believe in luck or in circumstance. Strong men believe in cause and effect."

40

"Our chief want is someone who will inspire us to be what we know we could be."

41

"A hero is no braver than an ordinary man, but he is brave five minutes longer."

42

"People do not seem to realise that their opinion of the world is also a confession of their character."

43

"Let me never fall into the vulgar mistake of dreaming that I am persecuted whenever I am contradicted."

44

"Peace cannot be achieved through violence, it can only be attained through understanding."

45

"Guard well your spare moments. They are like uncut diamonds. Discard them and their value will never be known. Improve them and they will become the brightest gems in a useful life."

46

"Every artist was first an amateur."

47

"The creation of a thousand forests is in one acorn."

48

"You become what you think about all day long."

49

"Nothing is at last sacred but the integrity of your own mind."

50

"Envy is ignorance, imitation is suicide."

51

"To be great is to be misunderstood."

52

"The mind, once stretched by a new idea, never returns to its original dimensions."

53

"If the stars should appear one night in a thousand years, how would men believe and adore; and preserve for many generations the remembrance of the city of God which had been shown! But every night come out these envoys of beauty, and light the universe with their admonishing smile."

54

"It is easy to live for others, everybody does. I call on you to live for yourself."

55

"Most of the shadows of this life are caused by standing in one's own sunshine."

56

"Be yourself; no base imitator of another, but your best self. There is something which you can do better than another. Listen to the inward voice and bravely obey that. Do the things at which you are great, not what you were never made for."

57

"When friendships are real, they are not glass threads or frost work, but the solidest things we can know."

58

"Happiness is a perfume you cannot pour on others without getting some on yourself."

59

"The good news is that the moment you decide that what you know is more important than what you have been taught to believe, you will have shifted gears in your quest for abundance. Success comes from within, not from without."

60

"There is creative reading as well as creative writing."

61

"In my walks, every man I meet is my superior in some way, and in that I learn from him."

62

"Life is a succession of lessons which must be lived to be understood."

63

"Nothing external to you has any power over you."

64

"Sometimes a scream is better than a thesis."

65

"Few people know how to take a walk. The qualifications are endurance, plain clothes, old shoes, an eye for nature, good humor, vast curiosity, good speech, good silence and nothing too much."

66

"The invariable mark of wisdom is to see the miraculous in the common."

67

"I hate quotations. Tell me what you know."

68

"This is my wish for you: Comfort on difficult days, smiles when sadness intrudes, rainbows to follow the clouds, laughter to kiss your lips, sunsets to warm your heart, hugs when spirits sag, beauty for your eyes to see, friendships to brighten your being, faith so that you can believe, confidence for when you doubt, courage to know yourself, patience to accept the truth, Love to complete your life."

69

"Trust thyself: every heart vibrates to that iron string."

70

"Sorrow looks back, Worry looks around, Faith looks up"

71

"Nature and Books belong to the
eyes that see them."

72

"That which we persist in doing becomes easier to do, not that the nature of the thing has changed but that our power to do has increased."

73

"The ornament of a house is the friends who frequent it."

74

"Let us be silent, that we may hear the whisper of God."

75

"Nothing can bring you peace but yourself. Nothing can bring you peace but the triumph of principles."

76

"People only see what they are prepared to see."

77

"Do the thing you fear and the death of fear is certain."

78

"In a library we are surrounded by many hundreds of dear friends imprisoned by an enchanter in paper and leathern boxes."

79

"You have just dined, and however scrupulously the slaughterhouse is concealed in the graceful distance of miles, there is complicity."

80

"For everything you have missed, you have gained something else, and for everything you gain, you lose something else."

81

"Life is short, but there is always time enough for courtesy."

82

"All my best thoughts were stolen by the ancients."

83

"You are constantly invited to be what you are."

84

"A foolish consistency is the hobgoblin of little minds."

85

"Some books leave us free and some books make us free."

86

"Common sense is genius dressed in its working clothes."

87

"Even in the mud and scum of things, something always, always sings."

88

"Nothing can bring you peace
but yourself."

89

"None of us will ever accomplish anything excellent or commanding except when he listens to this whisper which is heard by him alone."

90

"He who is in love is wise and is becoming wiser, sees newly every time he looks at the object beloved, drawing from it with his eyes and his mind those virtues which it possesses."

91

"Of all the ways to lose a person, death is the kindest."

92

"Life is a series of surprises and would not be worth taking or keeping if it were not."

93

"We are always getting ready to live but never living."

94

"Insist on yourself; never imitate. Your own gift you can offer with the cumulative force of a whole life's cultivation, but of the adopted talent of another, you have only an extemporaneous, half possession."

95

"Love, and you shall be loved."

"When you were born you were crying and everyone else was smiling. Live your life so at the end, your're the one who is smiling and everyone else is crying."

97

"Beauty without expression is boring."

98

"What is a weed? A plant whose virtues have not yet been discovered."

99

"The secret of education lies in respecting the pupil. It is not for you to choose what he shall know, what he shall do. It is chosen and foreordained and he only holds the key to his own secret."

100

"Whatever course you decide upon there is always someone to tell you that you are wrong. There are always difficulties arising which tempt you to believe that your critics are right. To map out a course of action and follow it to an end requires... courage."

Made in the USA
Middletown, DE
21 November 2021

53100623R00056